ART OBJECTS OF THE MAUNA KEA BEACH HOTEL

ART OBJECTS OF THE MAUNA KEA BEACH HOTEL

Selected from the more than 1,000 folk and museum art treasures assembled for the renown resort on the Big Island of Hawaii, a Rockresorts, Inc. property.

From the beginning, we planned and developed Mauna Kea Beach Hotel as a resort affording the visitor an experience in beauty as well as recreation.

To complement the spectacular natural beauty of Mauna Kea's Island of Hawaii beachside site, we sought out simplicity, spare elegance of form in architectural design. We wanted the hotel structure to enhance a flawless setting. We planned an open design to draw in and embrace the lush plantings, the soft air, the warm sunlight of Hawaii. We have attempted to make Mauna Kea appropriate to its surroundings.

Hawaii's orientation to the Pacific and its many peoples provided another inherent quality to imprint upon the evolving personality of Mauna Kea. An exhaustive and informed search yielded a collection of art objects to form a nucleus for the hotel's interior design. These pieces reflect the hotel's Pacific character, drawing upon primitive art, the Oceanic and Oriental folk arts and the enduring art of the ancient peoples of the Pacific Rim.

I hope that this book, presenting a selection of our decorative art objects, will enable guests to linger over the experience of Mauna Kea. For those who have not yet visited the hotel, the book will offer a sampling of the varied treasures that await.

LAURANCE S. ROCKEFELLER

TABLE OF CONTENTS

THE MANY WORLDS OF MAUNA KEA

The Many Worlds of Mauna Kea Beach Hotel encompass the lively spheres of championship golf on one of the world's best seaside courses, superb tennis, water sports, big game hunting, horseback riding on a vast Hawaiian ranch, world-famous sport fishing and more.

Just as exhilarating is the world of Pacific art, a world throbbing with the vitality of the new and the centuries-old — a multi-cultured tapestry reflecting the Pacific homelands from which the art objects come.

Among more than 1000 objects are a prized seventh-century Indian Buddha, a fearsome figure of the Garuda from a Thai temple, a 700-year-old Japanese Kamakura sculpture, brilliant batik tapestries from Ceylon, and primitive ancestral carvings from the New Guinea Sepik tribes.

Intriguing, sometimes amusing, occasionally awesome, the Mauna Kea collection invites further contemplation. Hopefully, these pages will beckon you to enter one or all of the many worlds of Mauna Kea Beach Hotel.

The Mauna Kea Beach Hotel, embraced by a championship golf course, enjoys one of the Big Island of Hawaii's finest swimming beaches. The flowing multi-tierred structure is a gallery of Pacific arts and artifacts.

THAILAND

The art of Thailand pulsates with a past as dramatic as the sound of a temple gong in the stillness of a Buddhist sanctuary. For Thai art serves a lively Buddhism, tinged with Hinduism and an animism culled from the cultures of the Mons and Cambodians.

Spirituality speaks out from the reverent Mokala, or follower of Buddha. In his original setting, the figure knelt in a worshipful group surrounding a large temple Buddha. Cast soon after 1782, when Bangkok succeeded decaying Ayudhya as the Thai Capital, the gleaming Mokala wears the opulent garb of gold leaf over black lacquer.

Big fish stories were never as rich as this gilded, elongated Thai fish. Once a temple offering, the fish now rests resplendent in an open court.

Pious hands carved this teak altar in honor of the compassionate Buddha more than 200 years ago. The elaborately-carved piece served as a stand for a temple Buddha sculpture. Later, when the temple was redecorated, painting was added, a scene dominated by the ascetic, red-draped Buddha, seated on the traditional lotus blossom. The five tiers now display tiny white vases filled with delicate baby anthuriums.

The Garuda, supporting figure in this 18th century Ayudhya teak sculpture, is friendly despite his disconcerting appearance—vulture legs, beak nose, monster pose. He is the Golden Bird, the unbound spirit of the Hindu literary classic, the Ramayana. He acts as the spiritual alternate for Phra Narai, the Thai version of the Hindu god Vishnu.

The Garuda dominated the main gable of a Thai temple, blazing forth in the brilliance of his glass mosaic dress to dazzle passersby.

A bronze ceremonial drum is from the 18th century Ayudhya period and has an artistic family tree that dates to 16th century China and Burma.

The guardian dogs once flanked the entry to a Thai palace or temple, their fierce features a threat to any evil spirits who might dare entry. Both male and female glitter with colored glass mosaic that dances in the sunlight. Made from bronze in the cire perdu (lost wax) process, the guardian dogs now add exotic punctuation to a promenade entry at Mauna Kea Beach Hotel.

Workmen building northern Thailand's Yanhee dam unearthed the damaged full figure of this 700-year stucco Buddha among the ruins of an old temple. The head, with its snail-shell canonical buddha headdress, reflects the inner quietude of the Buddha, purified and transformed.

When the message of Zen Buddhism was heard throughout Japan in the Kamakura period (1186-1333), the people turned from traditional ritual to meditation and simple, fraternal love of nature. The ear of the craftsman-artist opened up to the lovely internal melody of things. Then, in the crescendo of the arts that followed, came *cha-no-yu,* the harmonizing of life and beauty. Objects as simple as a barn hook or a cooking utensil sang out the beauty of *shibui,* a profound, quiet and unassuming spirit that underlies the best Japanese art. Moving to the beat of this new mood, a simple wooden fish gate knocker took on new spontaneity and freshness. The wooden fish, struck with a mallet, sounded the arrival of guests.

JAPAN

The Pacifica Bell Collection is a unique orchestra of gongs, temple bells and elephant bells, wind chimes and rattles from Japan, Ceylon, Thailand and Singapore. The chime at upper left once pealed out from the eaves of a Kyoto temple. The spherical flat kei gong near it was struck with a mallet during the recitation of sutras to the Buddha.

Zen Buddhism unleased a creative power that reached new heights of Buddhist sculpture. The Zen of the Kamakura period rejected the courtly mannerisms of the preceding Fujiwara era's art and loosened the strictures of time and tradition.

This Kamakura wooden figure utilizes a carving method, dan-zo, which releases the grain of the wood so that it ripples with the rhythm of the statue. Like many of the era's sculptures, this ascetic figure reflects the sublimity of Zen meditation.

Koi, the upstream-battling carp, is significant of the mysticism of early Shintoism, symbolic of perseverance. This bronze carp is one of a pair used to flank the entryway to the Dining Pavilion.

Heavy metal pots could be adjusted over the ro *(oven)* with these ingenious and beautiful jizai *(hooks),* used in an 18th century Japanese farmhouse kitchen.

Wooden lion dogs date from the 15th century Muromachi period when art became less religious, less intimate and more magnificent in scale than the preceding Kamakura era.

Contemporary calligrapher Morita Shiryu unfolds his own individuality in an ancient form in the red-on-black lacquer "sho" brush painting "A Dragon Knows Dragon." A ferocious figure to Western eyes, the dragon is, in the East, a blessed angelic being.

Gay antique wooden horse on wheels carried children during 18th century festivals. Tossing its colored tassels, the well-muscled little steed rolls his eyes, champs at his bit. Nigoro red Japanese tansu *(chest)* displays an intriguing carved stool from Dahomey. An old barn hook, simple as modern sculpture, embodies the concept of *shibui,* understated elegance, in the gleaming curve of burnished wood—quiet and beautiful. The mysterious Ainu, Caucasian-like peoples of the Northern Japanese island of Hokkaido, wove a wealth of mythological lore into the intricately-stitched coat displayed here.

INDIA

The art of India, as rich and copious as the country's own fertile abundance, emerges in a harvest of forms from whimsical folk art to the sublime and universal masterworks of Buddhist sculpture. The greatest Indian art sprang from the soil of Buddhism, yet in that same soil are the elements of Hinduism with images of Brahman, Vishnu, Shiva and a multiplicity of gods and goddesses and ancient mythology.

These bronze temple toys, marching in parade, reflect a myriad of artistic detail. The animal figures are symbolical links with the past. For example, the elephant once bore wings and roamed the sky, free as his celestial sister, the cloud. He lost his wings when he disturbed a saint at meditation and was cursed. The elephant shrank to subserviance, destined forever to draw men's carriages. Yet he still retains the power to attract the cloud and her life-giving rain.

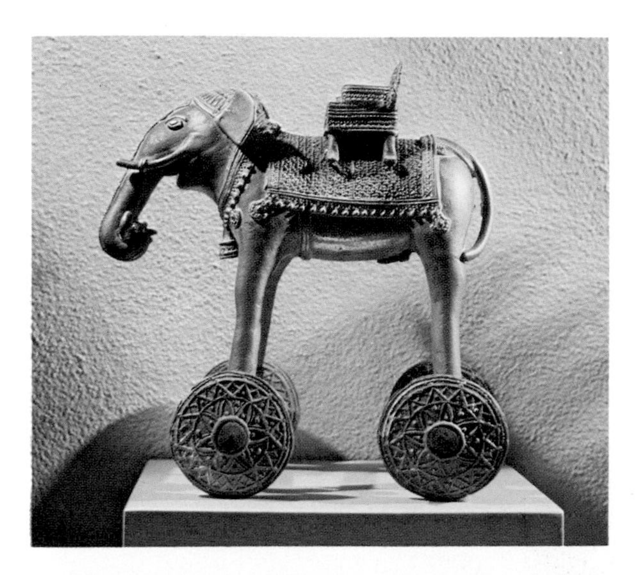

In another time and another world, the world of seventh century India, Buddhism held a continent in its calm and compassionate hands. At Nagapattinam, seedbed of Buddhist doctrine in South India, a sculptor, a devoted and visionary follower of the Buddha, began to chisel an image from the finest pink granite. As he worked he imparted life to the stone. Spirit and disciplined vitality seemed to flow forth from the frugal lines and planes of the face, the slim-torsoed, strong and radiant body. The five-foot three-inch seated Buddha exhibited the virile tension of yoga, a magestic presence, humane, awesome. The sculptor had created beauty and life from lifeless stone.

Nagapattinam declined in the eighth century. When the Hindu religion superceded Buddhism, this pink granite figure and three others *(one of them is now at the Chicago Art Institute)* were rudely overturned and half-buried to serve as cornerstone for a Hindu water tank. Every detail of the figure expresses the transcendence of the Buddha. The hands, poised in the traditional position of Buddha subduing Mara *(death and the passions),* remind one of Buddha's teaching that man is slave to his own desires and must subdue them. Buddha's radiance derives from the transformation of his whole being in the simple but permanent acceptance of life merged into the universal communion of truth. *(Technically, this radiance is enhanced through the Indian concept of "life breath" in sculpture. The sensuous rhythm of breathing out and breathing in flows through the form.)* The compassion that shines in the face of Buddha reflects his attainment of Nirvana, the extinction of individualized consciousness. He sits upon the lotus, the symbol of purity, the flower that springs up from the mud, but is undefiled. The lotus, associated with water and birth, is said to bear ripe fruit at the time it flowers—just as the truth of Buddha bears the immediate fruit of enlightenment.

The gleaming brass Chamla stored everything from rice to an Indian bridal dowry.

At Mauna Kea, these three-legged storage caches serve a decorative rather than a functional purpose, reflecting shafts of sun, foliage or architectural details in Lounge and Lobby conversational areas.

NEW GUINEA

Out of the primitive past, emerging from a dim tribal subconscious, comes the art of New Guinea. It is, surprisingly, as modern as the work of contemporary sculptors.

New Guinea, a damp, torrid land, larger than Louisiana and Texas together, is an isle of wide contrasts in race, language, custom. Explorers found its people in the Neolithic stage, using polished stone implements as recently as a century ago.

The powerful wooden sculpture dominated an entire village from the pinnacle of a Chawos tribe's ceremonial house. The man figure, with his scars of tribal initiation clearly visible, is carried by an eagle. The figure is a heroic emblem of the tribe.

The oval memorial tablet is linked in myth to the special guardian of its owners, and is thus consulted as an oracle. Beside it is an ancestor figure of carved wood probably created in the Maprick District.

A Sepik Valley house post carved with a human face, decorated a house tamburan *(men's ritual house)*. Human life in primitive New Guinea was held in the grip of the spirit world. This benevolent ancestor figure belongs to that world.

The mask of a tribal ancestor once cast its anxious gaze from the huge gable of a blackwater tribe ceremonial house, south of the Sepik. Plaited rattan is painted with lime, red clay, and ochre and black pigments.

Elongated wood-carved ancestor figure from a Karawari River ceremonial house is as modern as Giacometti.

Three hooked carvings seem to gather in a surrealistic dialogue with a Sepik Valley house post. The curious zoomorphic carvings, called Yipwon, represent a highly stylized version of the ubiquitous and mystically-endowed New Guinea crocodile.

Painted basketry masks are fashioned by village experts for adolescent initiation rites. The initiate then receives his superficial wounds, a blood-letting ceremony aimed to remove the boy's inherited female blood. He wears the face of plaited rattan to impersonate female ancestors.

These New Guinea war shields, like those brandished years ago by battling tribesmen in the southern Sepik, display vertically-arranged anthropomorphic faces with projecting tassel noses. Black cassowary feathers crown the shields. Red, yellow ochre, white and black highlight incised carving.

CEYLON

This land of enchantment proliferates with lively folk art. Like Hawaii, Ceylon was pliant under the shaping hands of many peoples—from India, most importantly, then from Holland, Thailand and across Asia. Craftsmen in the unhurried countryside of Ceylon still find ample time for crafts handed down through centuries. Batik, brasscraft, pottery, and wood carving are predominant among Ceylonese folk arts. The hand-worked pottery animals seen on these pages are sophisticated versions of a very old pottery craft. The Makara is probably the single most dominant non-Buddhist image in Ceylonese art: The Makara is a mythological creative figure which, in legend, spewed all the other animals from his mouth. The mouth is an alligator's, the nose an elephant's trunk, the paws a lion's, the tail a bird's, a fish's fin or a snake.

A four-tier brass column of light, handcrafted in Ceylon for the Mauna Kea Beach Hotel's Batik Lounge, is a contemporary creation in faithful reproduction of traditional Ceylonese brasscraft.

The ancient art of batik, ruled by codes of religion as well as form, traditionally somber in hue and sober in tone suddenly steps into today! These batik tapestries created by Ceylonese artist Mrs. Ena de Silva, are alive with color, animation, love of life and nature. A parade of peacocks, parrots and hornbills, elephants, butterflies and flowers march across tapestried walls of Mauna Kea's Batik Room and Batik Bar.

A native craftsman in the mountains near Kandy, Ceylon, charms travelers as he fashions these bright painted pottery birds and animals. Visitors help feed the fire or pass a tool while the folk artist turns out a delightful assortment of roosters, lions, horses, goats, and the symbolic Makara. The unpainted Makara figure in niche at upper left sports the often-seen fish tail.

TAIWAN A jaunty Chinese junk, made from teak in Taiwan, will never roam the high seas in search of adventure. The gay red sails could never buck the winds. Nor could the vessel handle the swells. The model, only five feet long, is anchored over the Cafe Terrace bar at Mauna Kea Beach Hotel.

TUNISIA White wire cages in scrollwork design make airy homes for island talking birds. Among them, Java rice birds, finches, German roller canaries, the half-moon parrot and peach-face love bird. Decorating the Garden Courtyard at Mauna Kea, the cages have gay red, green and white color accents.

CAMBODIA The ancient kingdom of Khmer, encompassing the present Cambodia and parts of Laos and Vietnam, flourished from the seventh to the 17th centuries. Khmer art is Buddhist in feeling, yet innovative, fresh. This 13th-14th century sandstone sculpture of a high official or priest, in the classic headdress of Khmer art, is a rich relic of a now-lost civilization.

ZANZIBAR An antique Arabic chest from Zanzibar displays elaborate brass hardware, fittings and hobnail work across face and top surfaces. The beautifully-grained wooden chest equipped with three small drawers provided years of service to its owners far across the globe; now its role is purely decorative.

The sun-blessed islands in an azure Pacific gather many peoples to their shores. From the Polynesian pioneers through the New England missionaries to today's new arrivals, these peoples add creative energy to Hawaii's arts.

Polynesians brought the art of tapa-making and design to Hawaii. Hawaiian tapa cloth, fashioned from the bark of the mulberry tree in seamless four-by-seven foot widths, is hand-imprinted with age-old designs. Until Laurance S. Rockefeller commissioned the creation of 14 authentic Hawaiian tapas for the Mauna Kea Beach Hotel in the mid-1960's, the art had been lost for 100 years. Exhaustive research and experiment by Honolulu's Malia Solomon uncovered the proper vegetable dyes, bamboo implements and patterns. Unable to duplicate the ancient method of making the cloth, Mrs. Solomon bartered personal possessions to secure the 14 antique and undyed tapas she needed. Below is one of the highly geometric, delicately designed Hawaiian tapas she produced.

HAWAII

The Bumpei Akaji sculpture depicts birds coming to rest at Mauna Kea, a "Kahi Hoakaokoa Hauoli" *(Happy Gathering Place)*. A group of Hawaii residents commissioned the work as a gift to Mr. & Mrs. Rockefeller.

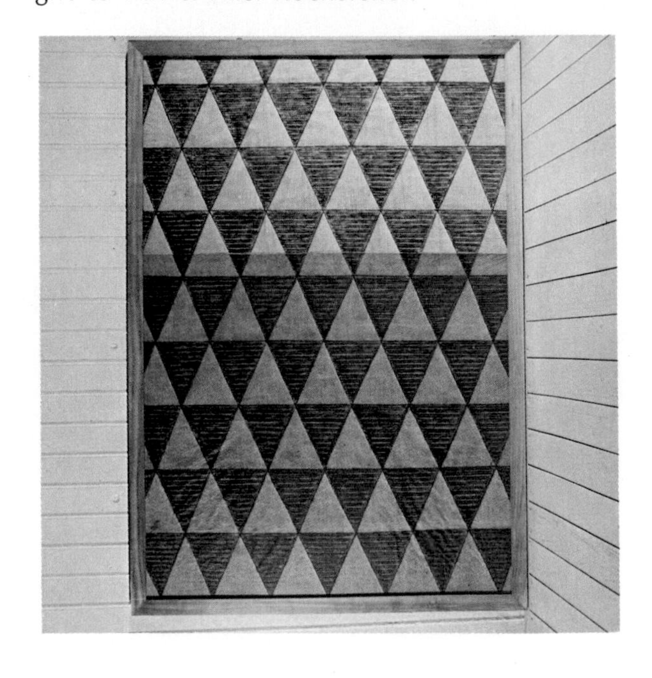

Hawaiian women had never seen a needle and thread until Spring, 1820, when the missionary brig Thaddeus stopped at Kohala, Hawaii, and several *alii wahine* (women of royalty) sat in on a quilting bee. In time, the Hawaiian women adopted—and adapted—the craft as their own. Their pattern designs, closely guarded and cut free-hand, tell a story of Hawaii's fruits, flowers, leaves, marine life, landmarks and legends. The Hotel's heirloom collection of 30 needle-perfect quilts revitalized public interest in the century-old, near-extinct art form. Each quilt contains two million stitches and took 1,000 hours to finish.

Under the direction of Mealii Kalama, five senior quiltmakers from Honolulu's Kawaiahao Church created the Mauna Kea quilts and tithed their commission fee to the Church, which is often called the Westminster Abbey of Hawaii.

CREDITS This book was produced for Mauna Kea Beach Hotel and Rockersorts, Inc. under the direction of Communications-Pacific, Inc., Honolulu. Text by Mary Ellen Gilliland. Design by Peter Sapasap and Paul Turley. Photography by Jerry Chong and David Cornwell. Edited by Bobbye Hughes. Printed by Kyodo Printing Company, Japan.